DEAD RABBITS

By Kate O'Dell

DEAD RABBITS

Kate O'Dell ©2021

WHO WERE THE DEAD RABBITS?

You may be wondering what the 'Dead Rabbits' are, and why they have such a funny name. 'Dead Rabbits' was the name of an Irish-American Catholic criminal street gang, that had been active in Lower Manhattan from the 1830s to the 1860s. The gang was also known as the 'Mulberry Boys', or 'Mulberry Street Boys' by the NYPD, because they worked along Mulberry Street, in the Five Points.

This book will take a look at the history of the 'Dead Rabbits' gang – the key players, how they formed, and how the gang got its name. There are also sections in the book about the 'Dead Rabbits' riot, as well as an image gallery at the end of the book. Firstly, a brief look at how many of the gang members ended up living in the Five Points, travelling across the ocean in search of a better life.

From 1845 to 1852, Ireland suffered a massive devastation with the Irish Famine. It was a time of mass starvation and disease, that led to a quarter of the country's population dropping – from nearly a million people dying, or from the high numbers of people emigrating to another country. Between one and two million people left Ireland, traveling on packet ships, barks, and steamboats. It was considered one of the greatest mass exoduses from a single island in history.

One of the main reasons why people were leaving in such large numbers, was because of the famine, caused by potato blight. Crops were infected throughout Ireland, as well as other parts of Europe. The famine, as well as British Whig government's laissez-faire capitalism economic policies, as well as absentee landlordism, and single-crop dependence meant that the Irish people suffered horrifically.

Many of the newly-landed immigrants went to Canada, which was under British rule. Others settled in the United States – in large cities like

Philadelphia, and New York. In the decade that Ireland suffered with the potato blight, almost a million Irish emigrants entered the port of New York. By 1855, nearly a third of the city's population were Irish-born, and by the end of the 19th century, New York was considered the largest urban Irish settlement in the world. Many newly-landed Irish families had very little money, and so they often settled in the city where the ship landed.

While many large American cities were welcoming towards immigrants, there were many New Yorkers that held anti-immigration sentiments. Tensions were running high, and a great deal of gangs rose up. Some of them, like the Bowery Boys, were *nativist* gangs – meaning that they only wanted native New Yorkers to live there, instead of immigrants. Other gangs, like the Irish Dead Rabbits gang, were pro-immigration, and took to fighting with any gangs who thought lesser of people just for originating in another country. They fought against the xenophobic English American Protestants, angered that they were not fully accepted in their new country, and frustrated with the conditions in which they lived.

Joining an Irish gang appealed to a great many newly-landed immigrants, because after they had fled poverty-stricken Ireland (which was dealing with a horrible famine), the Irish were looking to make a better life for themselves and their families. But upon arriving, many of them found themselves living in dirty, dangerous tenement slums, and often found it difficult to find employment. Joining a gang like the Dead Rabbits would have looked quite appealing to many in the area. The gangs gave them a sense of community, as well as a sense of stability.

The Dead Rabbits' founding location was Five Points, Manhattan. Its present-day location is Worth Street, Baxter Street, and Columbus Park. The gang had a great deal of allies: Chichesters, Tammany Hall, Roach

Guards, Plug Uglies, Municipal Police, Mulberry Street Boys, Forty Thieves, Kerryonians, and the Shirt Tails.

Their rivals were: Bowery Boys, Atlantic Guards, American Guards, O'Connell Guards, Empire Guards, True Blue Americans, New York City Police Department, and Simon City Royal's.

The Dead Rabbits would often commit robberies. The Bowery Boys, many being volunteer firemen, would often clash with other fire companies on who would fight which fires. There had been times where rival gangs would purposely set fires (knowing about the Bowery Boys' day jobs), and would attack the gang when they showed up to extinguish the flames.

The Bowery Boys also held day jobs as carpenters, and butchers. This meant that they financially had a leg up from the Dead Rabbits, as many of the newly-landed immigrants had very little money. William Poole (AKA 'Bill the Butcher'), worked as a butcher during the day in his family's shop.

In later years, many of the Bowery Boys went into politics – with jobs in the city council, and state legislature. Leader Mike Walsh was elected to Congress during the 1850s, in his desire to improve life in the slums where he had grown up.

It is believed that their name originates from the Irish phrase '*raibead sach ur*', which translates into 'fat cats'. Others believe that they were the 'rabbits', because of the Irish word '*raibead*' (it translates into 'to be feared'). With the word 'dead' being a slang word for 'very', their name 'Dead Rabbits' meant 'To be very feared'. Another theory, is one that concerns the Dead Rabbits gang. The Irish word *ráibéad* means 'big, hulking person'. Five Points had their own slang, and 'rabbit' meant 'a rowdy', and 'dead' meant 'very'. Tyler Anbinder (historian from the

George Washington University), believes that there was never any gang called Dead Rabbits.

There is, however, a well-known story of how the Dead Rabbits got their name. They first received the unusual name of 'Dead Rabbits', when the group was having a gang meeting, and things had become heated. During the argument, someone threw a dead rabbit into the middle of the room. Some of the members became quite frightened, seeing the dead rabbit as an omen, and so they split from the group to form their own independent gang.

The gang used the image of a dead rabbit on a pike, as their battle symbol. Some would nail dead rabbits outside of their home to signify their gang allegiance, as well as a way of scaring off their opponents. They would often spear dead rabbits onto a pike, and hold them up as they went into battle.

The Dead Rabbits would often clash with Nativist political groups (groups who were in favour of 'native' citizens, as opposed to immigrants. These nativist gangs would often support immigration-restrictive measures). Nativist groups saw Irish Catholics as less-than, and believed them to be threatening, and criminals.

The Dead Rabbits, were founded by two people – John Morrissey, and Shang Allen. Morrissey was an Irish boxer, who would later become a US Congressman. Shang Allen had been in the Roach Guards gang, and was one of the disgruntled members who left to form their own gang.

The Bowery Boys were the opposite of them in many ways – they were anti-immigration, anti-Catholic, anti-Irish, and they came from money. The group had been formed by William Poole (Bill the Butcher), and it had been formed specifically to stop immigrants from taking over the neighbourhood.

The Dead Rabbits also went by another name – 'Mulberry Boys', or 'Mulberry Street Boys'. This nickname was given to the gang, by the New York City Police Department, because the gang operated on Mulberry Street, in the Five Points.

The original members of the Dead Rabbits, had been disgruntled members of the Roach Guards. They had become the largest Irish crime organization in the early nineteenth century Manhattan, with over a hundred members. Their main rivals, were the Bowery Boys – a New York Nativist gang, that supported the 'Know Nothing' anti-immigrant political party.

The Roach Guards were an Irish criminal gang from the Five Points neighbourhood, in the early nineteenth century. They had originally formed to protect New York liquor merchants in the Five Points. However, they soon became a criminal gang – and started committing robberies, and murders. They got their name from their founder, Ted Roach.

The Roach Boys fought in 'Slugger Battles' against the Bowery Boys, and often the clashes would get violent when they fought over the Five Points area. Though they were not as organized or disciplined as the Bowery Boys, the Roach Guards held their own in a fight. The gang started to decline during the 1850s, however, and by the end of the American Civil War in 1865, the Roach Guards had disappeared entirely.

The Dead Rabbits and the Bowery Boys fought more than two hundred gang battles in a ten-year period (which started in 1834). Gang members often outmanned the police force, and even the state militias, and so it was difficult for the authorities to control them. They were prominent players in the Dead Rabbits Riot of 1857, and was believed to have participated in the 1863 New York Draft Riots in the American Civil War. The Dead Rabbits were able to call upon more than a hundred members to join in a fight against their opposing gangs, or to influence voters during elections.

Though the Dead Rabbits were known for their street fighting, the Dead Rabbits were also involved in local politics. They supported politician Fernando Wood (a Democrat, who served as the 73rd and 75th Mayor of New York City). Wood's platform was about the welfare and benefit of immigrant groups and minorities. Wood was heavily supported by Irish immigrants, who had travelled across the Atlantic Ocean, to escape the Irish famine.

It is important to note that many of the gangs in neighbourhoods with high immigrant populations (such as Five Points), were mainly men and women from the neighbourhood tenements, and not professional gangsters. A great deal of the gang members held jobs such as labourers, or shopkeepers during the day, and would be called on during elections to act as muscle for the local 'ward heeler' (a street-level boss who would work for Tammany Hall, or other political machines).

The biggest gang clashes were often politically motivated, as the gangs would be hired on by rival candidates to fight for control over the same street of voters. Contrary to what some films or accounts would show, most gang members would not be armed with swords or hatchets to murder their enemies.

By 1866, most New York newspapers referred to the Dead Rabbits in the past tense, as they weren't considered an organization currently in existence. By the 1880s, the term 'Dead Rabbits' had taken on a different meaning than the original gang. It became a generic term for a young, lower class criminal.

Isaiah Rynders (an American businessman, underworld figure, and political organizer for Tammany Hall), would often hire various gang members (or 'sluggers'), to commit voter intimidation, and election fraud. For twenty-five years, he held such a great deal of influence on Tammany Hall, that he was credited for securing James K. Polk's election as President of the United States. He also successfully helped Franklin Pierce, and James Buchanan.

He used a variety of different gangs for his own political reasons – such as the Dead Rabbits, and his many lieutenants (including Country McCleester, Jim Turner, Lew Baker, and John Morrissey) to go up against the Know Nothings, the Bowery Boys, and the Atlantic Guards.

Rynders was also alleged to have instigated the Astor Place Riot in 1849, which took place at the Astor Opera House in Manhattan. The riot left between 22-31 rioters dead, and more than 120 injured people. It was a clash between immigrants and nativists, but also against the wealthy New York who controlled the city's police, and state militia.

The riot had the largest number of civilian casualties due to military action in the US at the time, since the American Revolutionary War. It led to the vast increase in militarization of police, as they started to receive riot training, and got bigger, heavier batons to control civilians.

There had been an argument between American actor, Edwin Forrest, and English actor, William Charles Macready, as they fought over who was better at their Shakespearean roles.

Isaiah Rynders had been considered the de facto leader of the Five Points street gangs by the late 1840s. Often times, he would have police meet with him, and request that he stop riots, or gang-related violence, when the police were unable to keep the peace. Rynders also stopped attacks against certain abolitionists like Frederick Douglass, as Rynders was anti-slavery.

For a brief period, Isaiah Rynders switched teams, and started to publicly support the Know Nothings. He renamed his political organization the

'Americus Club'. This sudden shift angered a great deal of Rynders' Irish supporters, as well as his protégé, John Morrisey.

During the Dead Rabbits Riot in 1857, Rynders was attacked, and had rocks thrown at him, when he tried to convince the different gangs to stop fighting. His reputation became tarnished, and he soon was replaced as political boss of the Sixth Ward. His protégé, John Morrissey, took over his position.

HELL-CAT MAGGIE

One of the most feared Dead Rabbits, was a woman known as 'Hell-Cat Maggie'. She had filed her teeth down to points, and wore claw-like brass fingernails into battle. Hell-Cat Maggie (1820-1845), was well-known in the Five Points District as a fighter, who was an early member of the Dead Rabbits gang. In the 1840s, she would fight alongside the Dead Rabbits (and other Five Pointers), going up against nativist gangs, such as the Bowery Boys.

Hell-Cat Maggie was one of the earliest female criminals in the 'Gangs of New York' era (and was mentioned in Herbert Asbury's 1927 book '*The Gangs of New York: An Informal History of the New York Undeworld*'). She has often been compared to other female criminals, such as 'Gallus Mag' (a six-foot-tall female bouncer at a New York bar called the 'Hole in the Wall), and 'Battle Annie' (the leader of the female auxiliary of the Gopher Gang in the 1870s).

Hell-Cat Maggie's character had been featured in the 2002 film, 'Gangs of New York'. The character, played by Cara Seymour, was a composite of Gallus Mag, Hell-Cat Maggie, and Sadie the Goat. Hell-Cat Maggie was also featured in Thomas J. Fleming's 2003 historical novel, 'A Passionate Girl'. There has also been an Irish whiskey named after Hell-Cat Maggie, through the Phillips Distilling Company – which advertises the woman's ferocity as a street fighter, and her life as a Dead Rabbit.

Herbert Asbury wrote the following about Hell-Cat Maggie: '*The Dead Rabbits, during the early forties, commanded the allegiance of the most noted of the female battlers, an angular vixen known as Hell-Cat Maggie, who fought alongside the gang chieftains in many of the great battles with the Bowery gangs. She is said to have filed her front teeth to points, while on her fingers she wore long, artificial nails constructed of brass. When Hell-Cat Maggie screeched her battle cry, and rushed biting and clawing the midst of a mass of opposing gangsters, even the most stout-hearted blanched and fled.'*

Some people theorize that Hell-Cat Maggie (as well as other criminals of that time period), were actually fictional characters created by Herbert Asbury, in order to sensationalize that time period.

Tyler Anbinder, a historian from George Washington University, specializes in 19th century immigration. He consulted with Martin Scorcese for hours on the film 'Gangs of New York'. They went through the entire script, so that he could check for inaccuracies. He believes strongly that there is no real person named 'Hell-Cat Maggie', and after scouring 19th century newspapers, he could find no mention of her.

PRIEST VALLON AND AMSTERDAM VALLON

Martin Scorsese's film 'Gangs of New York' featured a colourful group of characters. Some of these were based historical figures, while others were loosely based off historical figures – so much so that they were barely anything like the original. The director tried in some ways to make the film feel legitimate, but also took liberties.

In Scorsese's film, there are two characters that the film focuses on greatly – the father, Priest Vallon, and his young son, Amsterdam Vallon. In the film, Liam Neeson plays Priest Vallon, the leader of the Dead Rabbits. Leonardo DiCaprio played Amsterdam Vellon.

The Dead Rabbits went up against William Cutting's protestant nativist gang. The Irish called them barbarians, and hated all non-wasps. Priest Vallon was a gang leader of the Dead Rabbits, who was highly respected. He attacked Cutting, and nearly killed him. Instead, he put out one of his eyes, and let him live in shame.

In 1846, Cutting retaliated during the final battle to who would retain control of Five Points. The Natives defeated the Dead Rabbits, and Cutting personally went after Vallon, and killed him.

During the 1850s to the 1860s, the Dead Rabbits went underground. Many of the gang members joined the Natives. Priest Vallon's son, Amsterdam Vallon, had been spared by Cutting. As he grew older, Amsterdam sought revenge for his father's murder. He decided to infiltrate the Natives, looking for his opportunity to go after Cutting. In 1862, Amsterdam tried to assassinate Cutting, but unfortunately, he was unsuccessful. Cutting had only been wounded. He decided to exile Amsterdam for his actions.

For a few months, Amsterdam stayed in exile. After receiving a visit from Walter McGinn, he decided to fight for his father's cause. He hung a dead rabbit on a fence. Amsterdam went after corrupt policeman Happy Jack Mulraney (a former Dead Rabbits member), and secured McGinn's election as the new Sheriff. Cutting retaliated by killing Walter McGinn, as well as Vallon's friend, Johnny Sirocco.

During the New York draft riots in July 1863, Vallon and the Dead Rabbits fought against the Natives. Many of the gang members died – some at the hands of other gangsters, others by the US Army.

But in the end, the natives were defeated, and Amsterdam Vallon was finally successful at killing Cutting. From that point, the Dead Rabbits were the main gang in the neighbourhood. But as time went on, the Natives, the Dead Rabbits, and other gangs were no longer as relevant as the city expanded, and buildings were torn down. The city changed drastically, and many of the structures that once stood, are no longer standing.

It is an epic story, full of revenge, and murder. But how much of it was historically accurate? Take the two main characters. Priest Vallon, and his son, Amsterdam. Were they real? It's likely not the case. Neither was William Cutting. It is believed that Priest Vallon's character was based on real-life person John Joseph Hughes, who was the archbishop of New York. Cutting, was a fictionalized version of William Poole (AKA 'Bill the Butcher').

John Joseph Hughes (who also went by 'Dagger' John Hughes). He was born on June 24, 1797, and was a prelate of the Roman Catholic church. He was the fourth Bishop, and the first Archbishop of the Archdiocese of New York (where he served from 1842, until his death in 1864). He was the founder of St. John's College, which later became Fordham University.

Hughes immigrated to the states in 1817, and became a priest in 1826. In 1838, he became a bishop. Hughes had come from County Tyrone, and was considered a champion of the Irish. Catholicism was growing at a huge rate in the United States, likely because of the waves of immigrants arriving in droves. Many considered Hughes to be the best loved Catholic bishop in the country. He received the nickname 'Dagger John', because of the Catholic practise where a bishop precedes his signature with a cross. Others called him that because of his aggressive personality.

Hughes held off anti-Catholic riots in 1844, as nativist rioters kept trying to burn down Catholic churches. Hughes had put armed guards in front of the churches to protect them. Hughes had said the following: '*If a single Catholic Church were burned in New York, the city would become a second Moscow.*' New Yorkers took Hughes' threats seriously, as they knew he meant business. The nativists were not allowed to hold their rally.

Hughes believed in education as being incredibly important, so that fellow Irish immigrants could take advantage of the endless possibilities in the states. With the right education and ton of hard work, one could bring themselves out of poverty, could move up in the world from the freezing, mosquito-infested tenements in Five Points, where people starved, and the buildings had shifting foundations from the filled-in marshy ponds.

He also didn't look too fondly on slavery, but had often noted that the condition of labourers in the states (particularly in the north), were not much better (and even were sometimes worse). In Hughes' opinion, he believed that abolitionists should advocate not just for slaves, but also for northern labourers. John Hughes died on January 3, 1864.

Many believe that the character of 'Amsterdam Vallon', was based on John Morrissey, leader of the Dead Rabbits who went up against William

Poole quite often. Morrissey was a boxer, who after retiring, went on to become Congressman.

William Poole ('William Cutting' in the film), was portrayed by Daniel Day-Lewis. There was no way that he could've historically attended the 1863 Draft Riots, as he had died in March 1855. There was no way he could've been at the riots.

JOHN MORRISSEY

John Morrisey, one of the Dead Rabbits' founders and gang leaders, was a champion prizefighter. He also went by the name 'Old Smoke'. He was born in 1831, in Templemore, County Tipperary, Ireland. His parents immigrated to the United States when he was only two years old, and they lived in Troy, New York.

Morrissey's father, Timothy, worked as a labourer to support his large family, as John had seven sisters. Morrissey only went to school for a short time, but by age 12, he started working at a wallpaper factory. Later, he worked at an ironworks, and then at a stove foundry.

By 1848, Morrissey started getting involved in setting up factional fighting in Troy between the Down-Town, and the Up-Town gangs. He was considered the kingpin at the time, who fought against Jack O'Rourke, the rival leader of the Up-Town gang.

That same year, he moved to New York, and started work as deck-hand on a steamer that ran from New York, to Albany. In 1849, he married the captain's daughter, Sarah Smith. He was still fighting, and had received a nickname 'Old Smoke' from one of these fights. One version says that he fought Thomas McCann, and that Morrissey had been pinned by McCann on pile of burning coals from an overturned stove. Despite the terrible pain as his skin burned from the coals, Morrissey was able to continue fighting. He managed to get back on his feet, and beat McCann to unconsciousness, even as his back continued to smolder from the burning flesh. This ensured that he was called 'Old Smoke', a name that clung to him throughout his life.

In 1851, Morrissey travelled to San Francisco, for the California Gold Rush. He was hoping to seek his fortune, but he was unsuccessful.

Instead, he became a gambler, making his fortune by winning gold from prospectors.

While in California, he made his first appearance in a professional prizefighting ring. The fight was against George Thompson, on August 31st, 1852. It took place on Mare island, California, and Morrissey defeated Thompson in the 11th round – winning a grand sum of $5,000.

Morrissey was pumped up from his fight against Thompson, and so he decided to make his return trip to New York and challenge 'Yankee Sullivan' (American boxing champion), to a match. Morrissey went to Sullivan multiple times, demanding that they fight, until Sullivan finally agreed.

Boxing was illegal in most places during the 1850s, because of its violent nature. The boxing rules had been put into place in 1743, by heavyweight champion Jack Broughton. The rules were made to protect fighters in the ring, as some boxers died from the sport. Fights were usually 20-30 rounds, and hits below the belt were prohibited. One could not hit a fighter who'd gone down, and if a boxer went down after a thirty-second count, the match was over. Rounds would continue until a fighter touched the ground with their knee, or if they fell down.

The articles for the fight between Morrissey, and Sullivan, were signed on September 1, 1853. Stake money was a thousand a side, and they were made clear that the London Prize Ring rules would be applied to their fight. Morrissey trained for two days with Orville Gardner, after signing the articles. On October 12, 1853, Morrissey and Sullivan fought in the hamlet of Boston Corners, Massachusetts – the perfect place for an illegal match, as it was out of the way of police. They fought in a field, surrounded by more than 3,000 spectators.

For most of the fight, Sullivan had the upper hand. He dominated, while Morrissey put up as good a fight as he could. During the 37th round, however, things quickly changed. There was a fight between the two players on the ropes created hostility between Sullivan and Morrissey's seconds, and the crowd broke out into a huge riot. Members of the crowd broke into the ring. The referee decided to give the decision to Morrissey, though some people present were unclear as to how he'd decided to make that verdict. Some thought that it was because Sullivan had struck Morrissey with a foul blow, while others thought that it was because Sullivan had stepped out of the ring before the referee had made his decision. In total, the fight had last for 55 minutes.

Though Morrissey had been elated about defeating Yankee Sullivan, he had to deal with the legal retribution for the fight. The Grand Jury of Berkshire County made a bill against him, and after surrendering to the court, Morrissey was fined $1,200.

He would later become the Democratic State Senator, and a member of the US House of Representatives. He was a noted actor, who rose up the political ranks to become state senator, and later, was a US Congressman, who strongly represented his Irish Catholic constituents.

John Morrissey was hired to go up against William Poole 'Bill the Butcher' – a notorious nativist enforcer for the Know-Nothing Party (Native American Party), and leader of the Bowery Boys. Morrissey's job was to stop William Poole from seizing election boxes, and rigging the election. In exchange, Morrissey and the Dead Rabbit gang were allowed to open a gambling house with zero police interference.

William Poole was a skilled bare-knuckle boxer, who also worked as a butcher. Poole was from New Jersey, and his parents had moved to New York City in 1832 to open a butcher shop. He also worked with the Howard Volunteer Fire Engine Company #34 (Red Rover), on Hudson, and Christopher Street. William Poole hated the Dead Rabbits gang, in particular, he despised John Morrissey. He considered them his most-hated enemy.

On August 8, 1854, Poole and Morrissey fought on the corner of 'West and Amos-street'. They sparred for quite some time, until Poole had had enough. He threw Morrissey to the ground, and jumped on top of him. He fought dirty – gouging, biting, and punching him, until Morrissey finally conceded the fight to Bill the Butcher.

A few months later, Bill the Butcher was shot at Stanwix Hall – a saloon located on Broadway. His shooters were friends of Morrissey - Lew Baker, and Jim Turner. Poole died in his Christopher Street home, surrounded by his family. His last words were: *'Goodbye, boys. I died a true American.'* Morrissey and Baker were brought to trial for Bill the Butcher's murder, though they never served time. The charges were eventually dropped, after three trials ended with hung juries.

Though Morrissey loved being a champion boxer, he eventually retired. He ran for Congress, and was backed by Tammany Hall. Morrissey served two terms from 1867-1871, in the House for the 40th and the 41st Congress – and he represented the Congressional District. He was known for always looking for the interests of the Irish.

John Morrissey died on May 1st, 1878, at the age of 47. He'd contracted pneumonia. Following his death, the state closed all their offices, and flags were at half-mast. The entire State Senate went to his funeral in Troy, New York, which was held on May 4th. There were more than 20,000 mourners lining the streets to pay their last respects. He was buried in St. Peter's Cemetery, in Troy.

TOMMY HADDEN

Tommy Hadden was a notorious saloon keeper in the Old Fourth Ward, owner of a Cherry Street dive bar – an underworld hangout beside Dan Kerrigan's business. Tommy Hadden was also co-leader of the Dead Rabbits gang, along with Kit Burns. Hadden had a great deal of political influence in the city, and was often able to receive protection from city officials during his criminal career.

Tommy Hadden started out as a Paradise Square street tough, often brawling with rival gang members on the street. Over time, he worked his way up the ranks until he became the leader of the Dead Rabbits alongside Kit Burns in the 1840s. Eventually, the two leaders moved to the Fourth Ward, where they set up popular dive bars, and other businesses along the busy waterfront. Although they had moved, Hadden and Burns often visited the Five Points during the 1850s and 1860s, to lead the Dead Rabbits in various gang activity.

Hadden's dive bar, was located on No. 10 ½ Cherry Street. He also owned a sailor's home on Water Street. For twenty-five years, Hadden ran his Water Street boarding house - a 'Crimp House', which preyed on sailors. They would wait for unsuspecting sailors to visit the premises – and then they would rob, murder, or drug them. Some of the sailors would get Shanghaied, get drugged and put onto ships. When the drugs wore off, the sailors would encounter Captains, and their short-staffed ships. They would usually be out to sea, and end up having to work their way back home. The boarding house got a lot of business as it was located near the waterfront – and thousands of sailors were robbed, shanghaied, or murdered on the property.

Although Hadden and Burns had some degree of protection from getting arrested for their illegal activity (such as their shanghaiing of sailors), Hadden was arrested for fighting, and other violent crimes, due to his continuous involvement with the Dead Rabbits. One of these arrests, was for the 1852 street mugging, where Hadden killed a man named Kehoe. Late at night, Hadden and two other men had lured Kehoe into a dark alley off Liberty Street. Hadden then attacked Kehoe from behind, shooting him in the head. They stole Kehoe's gold, and ran off. Kehoe didn't die straightaway. He was found alive, and was transported to a nearby friend's house on Fourth Avenue. Kehoe succumbed to his wounds a few hours after the mugging.

Tommy Hadden was arrested for the man's murder, along with his two accomplices. During the Kehoe murder trial, his two accomplices were convicted, and Hadden was acquitted – even though the same evidence was used against all three men. Hadden was often able to avoid convictions in Police Courts, and he only appeared once before General Sessions. That was for the kidnapping of Robert Wallace (who was shipped out to sea). For that crime, he was given the shortest possible sentence of two years in the State prison. Judge Roosevelt stated that '*the evidence against Hadden appeared to be very slight, but as that was received and submitted to a Jury, the Court could not interfere*'. Hadden was given a stay of proceedings, and his bail was reduced from two thousand, to one thousand – allowing him to post bail until the decision was made by the Court of Appeals. Hadden never served his two years, and went back to his criminal lifestyle.

In total, Hadden only served two short terms in the New York State Prison. In June 1870, Hadden was arrested for grand larceny in New Jersey. He was sentenced to ten years in the New Jersey State Prison – which New Jersey, and New York both celebrated. The New York Times was critical of the city officials, who had allowed Hadden to get away with so much crime over the years, standing in the way of justice. Hadden served his time, and when he was released, he returned to the New York waterfront, and started to work as a bootblack (or 'wharf-rat').

By 1881, it was reported that Tommy Hadden was working on the City of Alexandria steamship.

Hadden was also one of the saloon keepers involved in the Water Street Revival scam. The scam was created by Reverend A.C Arnold – founder of the Howard Mission. He used the names of some of the more notorious saloons in the area (including John Allen, dubbed 'The Wickedest Man in New York'), and he claimed that Allen, Hadden, and the others had denounced their sinful ways, and were now a part of his congregation. Rev. Arnold would use their saloons for prayer meetings, and to sing hymnals. On September 11, 1868, Hadden held a prayer meeting in his Water Street Boarding house. No prayer meetings were held in his Cherry Street business.

Journalists became suspicious of these prayer meetings. The New York Times ran an exposé on the prayer meetings, revealing that the Reverend had had been paying a great deal of money to the saloon owners to rent their businesses for the meetings. The revival was quickly brought to an end.

Hadden was specifically named in the article, as the paper charged him with '*playing the pious with the hope of being secured from trial before the Court of General Sessions for having recently shanghaied a Brooklynite, and also in consideration of a handsome moneyed arrangement with his employers.*'

KIT BURNS

Kit Burns, one of the Dead Rabbits members, was a notorious saloon keeper. He was a prominent underworld figure, and during the 1850s and 1860s, Kit Burns co-led the Dead Rabbits gang alongside Tommy Hadden. They were the last-known leaders of the Dead Rabbits.

He was also known for the 'Rat Pit' – where people would host rat-fighting, and dog-fighting games for sport. He was also known for founding Sportsmen's Hall (the Band Box), that served as a popular Bowery sporting resort, and dance hall. It was a meeting place for the New York underworld in the Bowery, and Fourth Ward for about twenty years – until they were finally shut down by the ASPCA in 1870.

Kit Burns' birth name was Christopher Keyburn, and he was born February 23, 1831. He joined the Dead Rabbits when he was a young man. By 1840, Kit and Tommy Hadden were co-leading the gang. They had both started up their own businesses in the Bowery (Kit Burns opened the Sportsmen's Hall on Water Street).

It was a place with all sorts of different events held for entertainment. Illegal bare-knuckle boxing prize fights were held there quite often, but there were other sorts of events that involved animals. There was a 'rat-pit', where people would host dog-fighting matches, as well as rat-baiting (releasing large, grey wharf rats in the enclosed space for dogs to hunt down and kill). The terriers would often be starved for days before the event, and would be set against other dogs to see who would win.

Kit Burns' two favourite dogs had been stuffed and mounted over the bar. Jack, a black and tan-coloured terrier, had apparently set an American record by killing a 100 rats in 6 minutes, and 40 seconds.

Hunky, had been a champion fighting dog that had 'expired after his last great victory'.

Sportsman's Hall was a three-storey frame house. The entire first floor was the 'rat pit', set up like an amphitheater, with rough wooden benches used as seats. In the middle, was a ring surrounded by a three-foot high wooden fence. The building also had a special narrow doorway installed, that would lead to a small space that allowed them to protect against a police raid. Some said that it could seat 250 people, while others believed it could hold about 400.

Sportsman's Hall was home to a series of strange employees. Richard Toner (Kit Burns' son-in-law), went by the nickname 'Jack', or 'Dick the Rat'. He would often bite off rat's heads, or mice heads for a price. Ten cents for a mouse, or a quarter for a wharf rat. George Leese (AKA 'Snatchem'), would act as bouncer during the events, and also as 'bloodsucker' during prize fights. He would suck the wounds of the prize fighters to prevent blood loss, and that would allow the fight to go on as long as possible.

Sportsman's Hall was notorious, and had procured a reputation in the Bowery, as well as in Manhattan. James William Buel wrote the following passage in his 1883 book, 'Mysteries and Miseries of America's Great Cities': '*Sportsman's Hall was an eating cancer on the body municipal, and within its crime begrimed walls have been enacted so many villainies, that the world has wondered why the wrath of vengeance did not consume it. But with all its festering and mephitic odors and criminalities, together with its votaries of Jezebel and Nana Sahib, the proprietor prospered and waxed rich. His rat and dog pits were known far and wide, and nowhere could the molochs and thugs find such delectable divertissement as Burns' pits afforded.*'

Kit Burns was one of the saloon owners involved in the Water Street Revival. He was one of the people who had supposedly been reformed by religious leaders, and allowed prayer meetings to take place in his rat pit – for a high fee. Though he was reluctant at first (and had denied the offer several times), Burns did eventually rent out the building for one hour a week – for the hefty price of $150.

The New York World reported on such prayer meetings, and in September 1868, the reporter wrote the following about the prayer meeting at Sportsman's Hall:

'Burns later mocked the movement, calling it "sheer humbug" and said, in reference to John Allen's holding an evangelical meeting in his establishment, "I've known Johnny Allen fourteen years, and he couldn't be a pious man if he tried ever so hard. You might as well ask a rat to sing like a canary bird as to make a Christian out of that chap." *The general public became skeptical of these meetings at the "rat pit", and a public inquiry was made to investigate the relationship between Burns and the missionaries. It was Burns himself, however, that was the first to turn against them. He and the other Water Street dive keepers were angry and having been paid less than half what John Allen had received. One night, during a nightly meeting, he announced to reporters present that* "them fellows have been making a pul-pit out of my rat pit and I'm going to purify it after them." *Burns gave the signal, and his barman began pelting the congregation of* "ladies and clergymen" *with rats, while the regulars taunted the crowd with insults. Burns mandated a nightly show soon afterwards, and* "referred to his sacrament as one that 'ratified' the meetings." *However, the hall operated a few weeks before the police shut the building down.'*

Kit Burns' animal abuse activities were so notorious, that Henry Bergh (founder of the ASPCA), personally led a crusade against him. Bergh's efforts were rewarded, and he personally got to see Burn getting arrested for animal cruelty charges, as well as ensuring that the 'Rat Pit' was permanently shuttered. The building was raided on November 31, 1870.

Burns' business was considered the city's largest dogfighting ring, and on that last night, Burns had put up an advertisement for '300 rats – to be given away, free of charge, for gentlemen to try their dogs with'. This would be the last event held in the building, as Henry Bergh had seen the advertisement, and made a point to be present when the building was raided. Kit Burns, and everyone else involved in the 'rat pit', were all arrested on animal cruelty charges, as the law had passed in the New York state legislature four years prior to the raid.

Everyone was acquitted at the trial. Kit Burns, however, never went to court. He had developed pneumonia, and it became so severe, that he died on December 19, 1870, in South Brooklyn, New York. He was only 39 at the time of his death.

The funeral service was held at his South Brooklyn home, and was attended by a large group of street urchins, customers and staff of his dogfighting ring, his family, and his friends. His funeral procession travelled along Sackett Street, and then to Calvary Cemetery, where he was laid to rest.

After Burns' death, his son-in-law Richard Toner, and English rat-catcher, Jack Jennings, continued to run his Water Street business. The 'rat-pit' was closed down, and Sportsman's Hall was turned into a saloon. Burns' widow applied to the common council for compensation, because police had released a cage full of rats into the East River during their raid, as well as damages for a $100 bullpup that had been seized during the raid.

Sportsman's Hall still stands, and is the third oldest house in Manhattan (after St. Paul's Chapel, and the Morris-Jumel Mansion). Not a lot of the original structure remains, as it has been more than century. Now, the site is home to the Joseph Rose House and Shop, a four-unit luxury apartment building.

ASTOR PLACE RIOT

Isaiah Rynders (an American businessman, underworld figure, and political organizer for Tammany Hall), would often hire various gang members (or 'sluggers'), to commit voter intimidation, and election fraud. For twenty-five years, he held such a great deal of influence on Tammany Hall, that he was credited for securing James K. Polk's election as President of the United States. He also successfully helped Franklin Pierce, and James Buchanan.

He used a variety of different gangs for his own political reasons – such as the Dead Rabbits, and his many lieutenants (including Country McCleester, Jim Turner, Lew Baker, and John Morrissey) to go up against the Know Nothings, the Bowery Boys, and the Atlantic Guards.

Rynders was also alleged to have instigated the Astor Place Riot in 1849, which took place at the Astor Opera House in Manhattan. The riot left between 22-31 rioters dead, and more than 120 injured people. It was a clash between immigrants and nativists, but also against the wealthy New York who controlled the city's police, and state militia.

The riot had the largest number of civilian casualties due to military action in the US at the time, since the American Revolutionary War. It led to the vast increase in militarization of police, as they started to receive riot training, and got bigger, heavier batons to control civilians.

There had been an argument between American actor, Edwin Forrest, and English actor, William Charles Macready, as they fought over who was better at their Shakespearean roles. During this time, theatre was a huge entertainment and community event, and was one of the main gathering places in many towns and cities. Certain actors would have huge followings, much like modern day movie and TV celebrities.

Theatre-goers would often feel free to speak their mind at the theatre – not just their opinions of the key actors, but also their opinions on political matters. It was not a rarity for theatre riots to occur in New York. During the nineteenth century, American theatre was mainly dominated by British actors, and their managers.

Edwin Forrest was the first American star, and this great divide among his supporters was an early sign of the home-grown American entertainment business. The riot that occurred at Astor Place, had been slowly growing for more than eighty years – since the Stamp Act riots of 1765. This was when an entire theatre had been torn apart, while British actors were performing on stage. British actors toured around the US, and often found themselves targeted by angry and violent protesters with anti-British sentiments. This was especially true because they were so prominent, and there were not as many other visiting targets.

Forrest and Macready were both fine actors, but were considered specialists in Shakespearean roles, as Shakespeare was seen as an icon for Anglo-Saxon culture in the nineteenth century. Many authors and poets were heavily inspired by Shakespeare's works, and the bard's plays were loved by people of all social classes. Even people in the California Gold Rush, used to sit fireside and read out Shakespeare's plays – sometimes, even acting them out from memory.

And so, when the two Shakespearean actors got into their dispute, their friendship turned into a rivalry. Many considered Macready the greatest British actor of his generation, while others loved that Forrest was the first American theatrical star. Anglo-American relations of the 1840s was poisonous, and the media quickly picked up on the rivalry, and started to discuss it in publications in great detail, deciding which actor they preferred.

Although Nativist groups were strongly against immigrants (which included Irish-Americans), and the Irish-Americans were struggling with alienation from Nativists, and other Americans, the two groups had one common enemy – the British. Forrest and Macready became icons for their home countries, and for the opposing views of the American, and British theatre fans.

By the time the riots had broken out, both Macready and Forrest had toured their rival actor's country twice. When Macready toured America during his second tour, Forrest took it upon himself to follow him around the country, and perform in the same plays that Macready had performed in, to challenge Macready's performances. During this tour, many of the local newspapers supported Forrest's stage productions, as he was a 'home-grown' star.

During Forrest's second performance in London, his British fans were less receptive towards him in comparison to his first visit. Forrest decided that this was Macready's doing – he must've turned people against him. When Forrest attended one of Macready's 'Hamlet' productions, Forrest loudly hissed at him to show his displeasure. Macready announced that Forrest was a man without taste.

Things escalated even further, when Macready did his third and final American tour. During one of his performances, someone threw half a carcass of a dead sheep onto the stage.

Forrest was going through a rough patch in his marriage, and he eventually started divorce proceedings against his English wife for immoral conduct. On the day that Macready arrived in New York for his farewell tour, Forrest got the news that the verdict in his divorce was against him.

Forrest had started out on stage at the Bowery Theatre, performing for working class New Yorkers. Many of his audience members were from the violent Five Points neighbourhood of lower Manhattan, that had a large immigration population. They were fond of Forrest's performance

– preferring his larger frame and booming on-stage presence, instead of Macready's slighter frame and quieter voice. Because of his background, he had a great deal of connections with working class people, as well as with the gangs of New York.

The Astor Place Opera House had been built near Broadway, as it catered to the wealthier theater-goers. Astor Place was quite pretentious, insisting on dress codes of kid gloves, and white vests. This angered a great deal of working class theater fans, as it was seen as a provocation, as theater had been considered a meeting place for people of all classes.

Macready had been scheduled to perform 'Macbeth' at the opera house. It hadn't been able to survive a full season of opera, and was working under the name 'Astor Place Theatre'. Forrest was also scheduled to perform 'Macbeth', although he would be a few blocks away at the Broadway Theater.

On May 7th, 1849 (three days before the riot), Forrest's supporters went to the Astor Opera House, and bought hundreds of tickets – all for the top level. When Macready tried to perform 'Macbeth', he was forced to stop. Forrest's supporters threw potatoes, apples, lemons, shoes, rotten eggs, bottles of stinking liquid, and ripped up seats onto the stage. The performers tried to continue the play, but they were met with so much noise that they couldn't be heard over the crowd. People were hissing, groaning, and shouting. They yelled out things like *'Shame, shame*!', and *'Down with codfish aristocracy!'* Even with the audience tried to mime the play, to perform a 'dumb show' instead of audibly saying their lines, they were unsuccessful.

Forrest, however, had received a vastly different sort of reception at his performance. The audience cheered for him, giving him a standing ovation when he performed the line 'What rhubarb, senna or what purgative drug will scour these English hence?'

After Macready's failure of a performance, he announced that he would leave for Britain on the next available boat. However, he was talked out of leaving so soon, and asked to perform again. There was a petition signed by 47 New York's elite – such as authors Herman Melville, and Washington Irving. They told Macready that 'the good sense and respect for order prevailing in this community will sustain you on the subsequent nights of your performance'. On May 10th (the night of the riot), Macready took to the stage to perform 'Macbeth'.

The day of the riot, police chief George Washington Matsell told Caleb S. Woodhull (the new Whig mayor), that they didn't have enough manpower to control the crowds if a riot broke out. Woodhull called in the militia for assistance.

General Charles Sandford assembled the state's Seventh Regiment in Washington Square Park. They had mounted troops, light artillery, hussars, and 350 men. They would be assisting the 1oo police officers that stood outside of the theatre, as well as the police posted at the wealthy citizen's homes in the nearby area.

Captain Isaiah Rynders had begun making preparations for the upcoming riot. He had been a long-time supporter of Forrest, and had been involved in the May 7th attack on Macready's performance at the theater.

Rynders disliked the new Whig mayor, and he wanted to embarrass him. He decided that he'd distribute handbills and posters throughout the city – to saloons, restaurants, and other businesses. Rynders wanted working men, and patriots to attend a large gathering. The handbills had the message 'Shall Americans or English Rule This City?', and plans were made for where people should be deployed. Free tickets were handed out in great numbers for Macready's May 10th show.

The play was set to open at 7:30 PM, and by that time, the crowd had gathered to more than 10,000 people around the theater. Ned Buntline, a dime novelist who supported Forrest, was one of the more prominent men in the crowd. He worked as Rynders' chief assistant, and had aided in plastering the city with the handbills.

Buntline and his followers started to throw rocks at the theater, and fought with the police. Many of the protesters tried to set fire to the building, but was unsuccessful. Ticket-holders were being screened before entry, and they were able to weed out a great deal of audience members with anti-Macready sentiments.

The audience members were greatly upset with the crowds outside, and the heightened tension. The situation inside the theater was becoming aggressive, and so loud that Macready and the other actors tried to perform a miming 'dumb show' like they'd attempted three days before. This time, they managed to get through the show. Macready slipped out of the show afterwards, in disguise in hopes that he would not be noticed.

Police feared that they had lost control of the city, and so they called in the troops. They arrived at 9:15 PM. Instantly, members of the militia were attacked, and some were injured. The soldiers lined up, and started to warn the crowd to settle down. When that didn't work, they fired their weapons into the air. Then, they fired point blank into the crowd, killing innocent bystanders and rioters. Most of the casualties were working class, seven of whom were Irish immigrants.

By morning, there were dozens of injured and dead from the riot, who were laid out in shops and saloons. Family members – mainly wives and mothers – went to the businesses, and the morgue, searching for missing loved ones.

The *New York Tribune* described the riot in their newspaper. They said the following: 'As one window after another cracked, the pieces of brisk and paving stones rattled in on the terraces and lobbies, the confusion increased, till the Opera House resembled a fortress besieged by an invading army rather than a place meant for the peaceful amusement of civilized community'.

On May 11th, there was a meeting called in the City Hall Park. The meeting had thousands of attendees, and speakers shouted out that they wanted revenge against the authorities whose actions they held responsible for the fatalities during the riot. The crowd was again boisterous, and raucous, as the people got riled up in their anger and grief. During the meeting, a young boy was accidently killed because the crowd had gotten so riled up. The crowd marched up Broadway, heading towards Astor Place. They fought against the authorities, who were armed and hiding behind barricades. The authorities, however, managed to gain control of the situation, and stopped the crowd from getting too out of hand.

Though there are some discrepancies about how many were injured or killed during the riot, it is believed that there were as many as 31 rioters killed that night. There were also about 48 more rioters injured. About 70 police officers were injured, and about 140 militia were injured by the rioter's missiles. There were three judges who were involved with pressing for convictions after the riot was done. The elite wealthy New Yorkers heaped praise on the authorities, and their hard stance against the rioters.

After the Astor Place Riot, Ned Buntline was fined $250, and sentenced to a year in prison in September 1849. Upon his release, Buntline continued to write sensationalist stories for newspapers. He was involved in other riots, such as the nativist riot in St. Louis a few years later.

Astor Opera House didn't fare very well after the riot. It was given a great deal of nicknames by burlesque and minstrel shows, such as 'DisAstor

Place', and 'Massacre Opera House'. The Astor did try to run with another season, but with little success. The building eventually was turned into the New York Mercantile Library. The wealthy New Yorkers who had flocked to the Astor before the riots, soon found a new home when the Academy of Music opened up. It was a bit farther away, located uptown at 15th Street, and Irving Place. The elite believed that it was a better neighbourhood, as they wanted nothing to do with the working-class, or the rowdy citizens of the Bowery.

The new theater owner had learned a valuable lesson from the Astor Place Riot, and when the new venue opened up, it was no longer strictly keeping everyone divided by class as the Astor had done. Forrest's reputation was considered tarnished by some, though his acting style inspired a great deal of future actors. Early Hollywood actors, such as John Barrymore, took to the screens with heroic matinee performances, inspired by Forrest.

According to Nigel Cliff in 'The Shakespeare Riots', the Astor Place Riot had forced a greater divide between the elite, and the working-class citizens in New York City. This process of class alienation in America, further created a split between the sort of entertainment enjoyed by the opposite ends of the class spectrum. Vaudeville houses would perform Shakespeare, or skits based on the bard's plays. Professional actors would focus on 'respectable' theaters. Over time, Shakespeare's works were no longer considered material appropriate for people of all classes, but was set into a new category – highbrow entertainment for the elite.

STANWIX HALL CONFRONTATION

The leader of the Bowery Boys, was a man named William Poole (AKA 'Bill the Butcher'), and he was an enforcer for the Know-Nothing Party – a nativist organization opposed to the influx of Catholic immigrants. John Morrissey, an Irish immigrant, was the leader of the Dead Rabbits, and was associated with Tammany Hall.

On February 25, 1855, the two rival leaders had a confrontation at Stanwix Hall. John Morrissey and a few rowdy gang members, decided to visit a saloon at No. 579, Broadway. It was nine o'clock at night. Bill Poole was there that night, and the two men fought – until the bar owner brought in the police to break up their fight.

Three hours later, just after midnight, Morrissey and his men returned to Stanwix Hall to attack Poole a second time. They attacked him brutally, and Poole ended up on his death bed.

He was quoted as saying *"I think I am a goner. If I die, I die a true American; and what grieves me most is, thinking that I've been murdered by a set of Irish – by Morrissey in particular."*

William Poole died shortly after. Though he had been a brutal man, about a quarter of a million people filled the Manhattan streets to pay their respects to the dead gang leader.

DEAD RABBIT RIOT

At the time, New York's Democrats were split into two groups – supporters of Mayor Fernando Wood, and his opposers. The Bowery gangs opposed Wood, while the Dead Rabbits were in support of the mayor. The Bowery Boys decided to wholeheartedly support Republicans, as they'd proposed legislation that would strip Wood of much of his power, and place them in Albany's hands. One of these proposals wanted to disband the Municipal Police Department that Wood's supporters were heavily interested in, and instead replace it with a state-run Metropolitan Police Department.

Wood held out for a long time, refusing to disband the Municipal Department, and during the first six months of 1857, the two rival departments took their fight to the streets. In July, the courts ordered that the Municipals disband.

On July 4th 1857, a riot broke out between the Dead Rabbits and the Metropolitan Police, and the Bowery gangs against the Municipal Police, Roach Guards, Mulberry Street Boys, and the Dead Rabbits in Bayard Street.

The Bowery Boys, and the Dead Rabbits fought considerably over a small plot of land known as the 'Five Points district'. It got its name from the five-pointed intersection on the southeastern corner, that encircled a triangular-shaped plot known as 'Paradise Square'. The area was a grimy tenement slum that was considered the worst in the country, some saying it was the worst in the world. The tenement slum was home to immigrants, extremely poor people, and also the formerly enslaved.

The Bowery Boys believed that Paradise Square should be under their care, but the Dead Rabbits believed that it should be under their control. The two groups had different reasons for wanting control over the land.

Bowery Boys wanted to keep out the immigrants, forcing them to live elsewhere. The Dead Rabbits were keenly aware that a great many immigrants lived in the dangerous slums, as they were hard-working, but many had little to their name.

The fighting started on July 4th – American independence Day. It went on for two days. The Dead Rabbits had decided to lead a group of its members from Five Points, to the Bowery. They wanted to raid a clubhouse occupied by the Bowery Boys. Their raid was unsuccessful, and the Bowery Boys fought outside of the building, before driving them back to the Five Points. The police had decided not to get involved, and so the Dead Rabbits returned early the next day to continue fighting. They went after the 'Green Dragon', a Bowery Boys hangout.

The Dead Rabbits, who had travelled from Cow Bay to the Bowery (Nos. 40, and 42), attacked the Atlantic Guards, and the Bowery Boys. The Bowery Boys fought back – with clubs, stones, brick-bats, and guns). The Dead Rabbits were forced back, and retreated to their houses on Elizabeth, Mulberry, and the Five Points. They were shouting in the streets, and firing their revolvers into the air, making a great deal of noise.

Things took a turn for the worst, however, when the Bowery Boys called in reinforcements. As the fight escalated, there became more than a thousand gang member joining the fight. People were afraid to leave their homes, in fear of getting injured during the riots. During the second day of the riots, a group of rioters came to the corner of Worth and Centre Streets, into Cow Bay, and continued the attack on Five Pointers. This was met with great resistance.

Dead Rabbits decided to climb up onto the roofs of the houses, and ripped out the chimneys. They used the bricks as ammunition, throwing them down at the crowd of Kerryonians below, and handing out bricks to their fellow gang members. At one point, a Reverend Pease stepped in between the two groups, and removed a double-barrelled shotgun away from a Five Pointer. Other civilians stepped in, trying to keep the peace.

It didn't help matters any, when the two opposing police forces (Metropolitan Police, and Municipal Police), joined in, and started to riot against each other. The two groups of police had been clashing for quite some time, and had had their own riot against each other on June 16th of that year.

Outside of the old Sixth ward station house (located at 133 Walker Street), there was a battle between a group of men in Leonard, near Baxter Street. The police showed up to break up the fight, but instead of retreating, the group banded together to attack the police officers instead. The Metropolitan police were driven from the Sixth ward.

The police had gone to Tammany Hall political organizer Captain Isaiah Rynders, and asked him to negotiate a truce between the two rival gangs. He was unsuccessful, and he suggested to the police that they call in the militia to sort things out.

On July 5th, at 9 PM, the New York State Militia arrived on the scene. They marched down the New York streets, armed with bayonets, forcing their way through the throngs of fighting gang members and police. The Militia were never one to shy away from using their weapons to control the crowd. They clubbed people, impaled them with their bayonets, fought the crowds into submission.

The fighting eventually ceased, when the rioters retreated back to their hideouts. In total, there were eight known deaths, and about a hundred severely injured rioters. The number may well have been higher, though, as both the Bowery Boys and Dead Rabbits dragged off their injured members from the scene of the riot.

Following the Dead Rabbits Riot, tensions lessened in the Five Points area. There were still violent incidents between the two gangs, but nowhere near as it had been before. The gangs tended to keep to themselves. The Dead Rabbits considered this a partial victory. Though they had not managed to fully drive the Bowery Boys out of Five Points, they had managed to reduce their opposing gang's hold on the tenement slum.

Thought the initial clash was considered a small-scale riot between the Dead Rabbits, Bowery Boys, and the disorganized police force, things quickly got out of hand. Widespread looting, and property damage occurred, as gangs from the different boroughs joined in the riot. It was estimated that there were about 800 to 1000 gang members involved in the riot.

NEW YORK CITY DRAFT RIOTS

In 1863, in the second year of the American Civil War, Congress decided that they needed more men to fight for the Union. They decided to tighten their conscription – using a lottery system to choose men for the draft. All males between 2o-35, and all unmarried men between 35-45 years were subject to military duty.

The wealthy didn't have much to fear with this conscription. The law had a provision that if the rich person's number was called up for service, it allowed them to pay someone $300 to take their place. This provision meant that the rich could easily afford to stay out of war. But many New York residents had no way of paying that exorbitant price. In today's prices, that the $300 the wealthy were paying to avoid fighting in the war, would equal to just over $6000.

Working class, and immigrant people living in Lower Manhattan, thought that the conscription (and the provision) was highly unjust. They believed that it was just a way to keep the rich protected, and to send the poor to die on the frontlines of the war. The Irish, in particular, believed that the law had been built to target them specifically. Black men weren't even eligible for the draft, as they were not considered citizens of the United States.

The Irish were also angered that freed black people, were trying to steal jobs from them. They didn't like them, fearing that they would steal food from the mouths of their children. For the past few months, many black citizens had begun working at the docks in various positions. This angered a lot of people – as many believed that the black community didn't belong, and wanted them out of the industry. They also were upset, because with the new influx of workers, job scarcity was much higher, and the Irish were struggling with the job competition.

The enactment of the Emancipation Proclamation marked two years of anti-slavery support in New York City. At first, Republicans had tried to force out abolitionists from the city, but by 1862, there were a great deal of white and black abolitionists in the city that would draw huge audiences. It was, in fact, members of the Democratic Party (particularly the Irish), who were holding anti-slavery sentiments at that time.

For a few years before the Emancipation Proclamation had been signed (September 1862), the Democratic Party had warned New York's Irish and German residents to prepare for an influx of freed black people to move to the area, as they travelled from the southern states to New York. These Irish residents considered the Emancipation Proclamation to be a confirmation of their worst fears. Many white residents were distressed by the economic situation, and believed that the black population that had recently moved to the area were at fault. The Irish hated that their economic status was at risk, and that the freed black residents were taking too much power.

Tensions were running high. Wartime inflation made everything especially expensive, and the poor suffered from these inflated prices. People were feeling persecuted, There were a great deal of anti-black sentiment, as well as rage against the government.

New York's economy depended on the southern states. By 1822, almost half of its exports were cotton shipments – and New York had a great deal of business tied with their textile mills that processed cotton in manufacturing.

On January 7, 1861, Mayor Fernando Wood had asked that the city's independence be declared from Albany, and from Washington, stating that it would have the whole and united support of the Southern States. When the Union entered the war, there was a great deal of southern sympathizers in New York.

The month leading up to the July lottery, newspaper editors with anti-war sentiment published a great deal of provocative attacks on the draft law, which were aimed at spurring on the white working class. The newspapers wrote many articles, heavily criticizing the government's intrusion into local affairs. Many newspapers would purposely insert anti-black sentiments into their news stories, and also showed derogatory portrayals of black people to get as many people against the black community as they could. Newspapers would write about how black people were trying to get the vote, or a decent education, or steady employment – and they would mock them, speaking about these issues with great derision. They would also provide pseudo-scientific lectures on phrenology (the study of skull shapes to indicate one's mental abilities, which was used by some to justify slavery), even though it had been debunked by medical doctors.

From July 13-17, 1863, huge riots broke out through New York City, as the working-class fought back against the unfair draft to fight the Civil War. The Draft Riot became the largest urban disturbance in American history, and was racially charged as white rioters attacked freed black men, and the black community throughout the city. In total, there were more than a hundred people killed during the riot, and more than two thousand injured.

On July 11, 1863, was the first day that the conscription lottery was held. The draft selection process was random, and the balloting by electoral district under the supervision of provost marshal Colonel Robert Nugent, who had been injured in the battle of Fredericksburg in December, 1862. Nugent's plan was to do the draft in a rolling manner throughout the city – starting in the Ninth Congressional District (which was Manhattan, north of 40th Street), and then move on until he got to the poorer areas of the city. It was his belief that if there were trouble arising from the draft, it would be expected downtown, in the notorious slums of Five Points, and Corlears Hook. He had set it up in a particular way, hoping that any protest would only focus on a single draft office.

Saturday, the first day of the draft, was relatively quiet. Sunday was considered a day of rest, as many were extremely religious. Many businesses weren't even open on that day. It was also the anniversary of the Battle of the Boyne, and so many Catholic Irish were honouring that. Many New Yorkers stayed close to home that Sunday, as they sat in the sweltering heat – sitting on front stoops to talk politics with friends and neighbours, or going to the bar. Word quickly got around in saloons and tenements, that on Monday, people would be protesting the draft. It had been decided that shipyards, docks, and factories would close for the day in protest.

But by Monday, July 13th, the Draft Riot officially began. This was the second drawing of draft numbers, which took place ten days after the Union victory at Gettysburg. A great deal of factory workers, dockworkers, and labourers had stayed home from work to protest. Some showed up to work, to specifically demand that the factories be shut down for the day.

At ten o'clock the morning of the 13th, a mob of about five hundred people went to the draft office of the Nineteenth Ward, at the assistant Ninth District provost marshal's office (located at Third Avenue, and 47th Street). This was where the draft was supposed to take place. The crowd was led by the volunteer firemen of Engine Company 33 (known as the 'Black Joke'). Nugent, and the police commissioner were not expecting any trouble, as they had expected to simply begin the draft selection as planned.

But as the names started to get announced, the firemen from Company 33 stormed the draft office, and quickly started burning as many draft papers as they could find. The staff were terrified, and quickly ran from the building. The mob of rioters started to throw bricks and paving stones through the windows, and then forced their way through the doors. Some of the police officers on the scene were attacked, while the others ran, fearing they would be injured by the growing mob of angry protesters.

The crowd set the building on fire. When the firemen tried to fight through the crowd and extinguish the flames, the rioters destroyed the firemen's vehicles. Other rioters killed horses that were pulling streetcars, and smashed the cars until they were destroyed. They also cut telegraph lines, in hopes that the rest of the city would not be notified straight away that they had begun rioting.

The New York State Militia were in Gettysburg, assisting Union troops. This meant that the only available people to fight the riots, were the New York Metropolitan Police Department. John Kennedy, Police Superintendent, arrived on the scene of the riot on Monday to see just how bad the situation was. Even though he was not in uniform, he was still recognized. Kennedy was attacked by rioters. He was left nearly unconscious, with a cut-up face, an eye injury, swollen lips, and a stab wound to his hand. His entire body was covered in bruises from the attack.

Nugent, who was at the Park Barracks, sent out a 32-member squad of soldiers from the Invalids Corps. The mob quickly attacked them, and two of them were killed. The police were quick to draw their weapons (clubs, and revolvers), and they tried to charge the crowd. They were outnumbered, and easily overpowered. Though they were not able to stop the riots, the police were able to keep the rioters out of Lower Manhattan, below Union Square. Certain areas (such as residents of the 'Bloody Sixth' Ward, the Five Points areas, and near the South Street Seaport) were not active in the riot.

The 19th Company and 1st Battalion US Army Invalid Corps (part of the Provost Guard) tried to break up the mob with gunfire, but they were also overwhelmed. They had one soldier missing (presumed dead), and fourteen injured.

The rioters travelled to the Bull's Head hotel (44th Street), and demanded that the hotel serve them alcohol. When the hotel refused, the rioters burned the building to the ground. They then turned their attention to the mayor's house on Fifth Avenue, but after Judge George Gardner Barnard spoke out, the crowd decided to spare the mayor's property, and turned their attention to other nearby buildings.

Two police stations (the Eighth, and Fifth District stations) were both attacked, and set on fire. Rioters also went after the *New York Times* office, but were surprised when staff members were armed with Gatling guns (a rapid-fire multiple barrel firearm invented in 1861, which was essentially like modern day's machine guns). One of the armed staff at the *Times*, was founder Henry Jarvis Raymond.

The crowd moved on to the *New York Tribune*, where they looted and burned the building. Some of the firemen that showed up to the riot were sympathetic towards the rioters, as their number had been selected during Saturday's draft. Police showed up, and did their best to put out the flames, while also trying to disperse the crowd.

The crowd didn't consist only of men. Onlookers later reported that they had witnessed women protesting as well, swinging aprons and handkerchiefs, cheering in the crowd, and encouraging the other protesters.

That afternoon, a man was shot by police, as rioters attacked the armoury on Second Avenue, and 21st Street. Rioters had smashed the windows with bricks, ripping up paving stones from the street to use as weapons.

New York had a great deal of armament factories, and rioters decided to target the Union Steam Works (which was only a block away from the gun factory on Second Avenue), the police had managed to garrison the factory, and fought off the rioters for as long as they could. Eventually, the rioters managed to get into the building, but by then the police had already removed all the guns.

Rioters targeted military and government buildings, as they perceived them as being symbols of the unfairness of the draft. Angry rioters specifically targeted these government buildings, because they blamed it for the unfair draft. Buildings were looted, and then set on fire in retaliation. Rioters also fought against federal troops, and the police. They attacked Republicans, and wealthy people, enraged that they were able to buy their way out of the war. Mobs had attacked civilians, going after people who they saw as enemies, or those who took a stand against the rioters.

Rioters started to search for wealthy people on the streets, targeting people that were well-dressed. They would shout out 'Down with the Rich!', or 'There's a $300 man!' when they saw someone who looked like they came from money. Some of them were attacked and beaten. Soldiers in uniform (as well as on leave) were also attacked on sight. The rioters asked a few people for anti-Republican speeches, or demanded that they buy a round of drinks.

By the afternoon of the first day, some of the rioters decided to go against the black population – as they saw them as symbolic of black political, economic, and social power. Freed blacks became scapegoats for the Irish people's anger, and a great deal of the rioters took all their rage and frustration out on black citizens. Many black people were murdered, or heavily injured during the Draft Riots. One of the first attacks, was a fruit vendor, and a nine-year-old boy working on the corner of Broadway and Chambers Street.

Rioters also burned down an orphanage for black children (the *Colored Orphan Asylum*), on July 13th, the first day of the riot. The Colored Orphan Asylum, was on Fifth Avenue. It was a financially stable orphanage that was kept well-stocked with food, clothing, furniture, and everything that was needed to care for the children living on the premises. Many saw the tall building as a symbol of white charity towards the orphaned black children, and were angered by what it stood for, and that the black children would live comfortably, while working-class people were barely able to scrape by.

The orphanage had been considered a model institution before the Civil War. The razing of the orphanage was a huge loss to the community, as the orphanage had cared for more than two hundred children, and was mostly run by women. It had been located on Fifth Avenue (between 42nd, and 43rd Streets, in Midtown, Manhattan). The four-storey building had had two wings. Founded by Quakers, it had been the first of its kind when it opened in 1836, caring for orphaned children, or for children whose parents couldn't care for them. There were also Indigenous children housed at the orphanage, too. Before it had opened, the black orphaned children had been placed in jail, or worked as beggars, or chimney sweeps, because orphanages refused to take them in. Many of the orphans were only given a small amount of education, and by age twelve, they were placed in homes or farms into an indentured servitude until they turned twenty-one. Some were returned to families, if the parents were deemed fit to care for them again.

There were 233 children living in the orphanage at the time of the riot. By four o'clock that afternoon, a mob of several thousand men, women, and children attacked the orphanage with bats, bricks, clubs, and any weapon they could get their hands upon. The children had been resting in the orphanage's infirmary, playing in the nursery, or doing schoolwork in their classrooms when the mob attacked.

The mob tore through the orphanage, stealing food, bedding, clothes, furniture, books – anything they could carry away with them. And when they were done looting, some of the mob set the orphanage on fire. Within twenty minutes, the building was completely gutted. Even though there were firemen on hand (including chief engineer John Decker), there was nothing they could do to salvage the building.

The children were thankfully spared death, as a policeman helped the orphans escape out the back door during the fire, though he was killed while helping them. The superintendent and matron of the orphanage quickly helped lead the children out of the building, to 44th Street.

The mob didn't attack the children. One Irish member of the crowd called out 'If there is a man among you, with a heart within him, come and help these poor children!' This angered the crowd, and they quickly grabbed the man and started to attack him.

The children and staff members walked up to the 35th Street Police Station, where they stayed for three days under police protection. After that, they were moved to the almshouse on Blackwell's Island – which was ironic, as the staff at the orphanage had fought to protect their wards for three decades, hoping to keep them out of such places.

After the riots, the Colored Orphan Asylum, which had been burned to the ground, tried to rebuild the orphanage on the same site as it had formerly stood. Nearby property owners, however, told them leave, and drove them out of the neighbourhood where they'd once been.

Instead, they relocated to 51st Street for a few years, before eventually finding its new home in 1867 on 143rd Street (between Broadway, and Amsterdam - in what would later become Harlem, a predominately black neighbourhood).

In 1907, it moved again – this time to Riverdale, Bronx. Though the orphanage had some issues with its condition, and many children died while living there, the place tried to give the children a decent home, and provide them with practical skills they could use after ageing out. With its later site in Riverdale, the children lived in cottages (25 children, and a housemother to each cottage), as they tried to give the children the best care possible.

The Irish man who had spoken up in support of protecting the black orphans, was not the only white person that was harassed and attacked by white rioters. The five-day riot saw a great deal of people deemed sympathetic to blacks get harassed for speaking up. Some had their property destroyed, others attacked.

There were a great deal of black men who worked at the docks, and they became vulnerable to attack, when tensions boiled over between black dock workers, and the white longshoremen. As of March 1863, white employers had begun hiring black men to work as longshoremen, and this angered Irish men so much that they refused to work with them at all.

During the raid, an Irish mob attacked two hundred black dock workers, angered that they had taken these dock jobs. Other rioters took to the streets, declaring that they were in search for 'all the negro porters, cartmen, and labourers that they could find'. The police were on scene, and they tried their best to intervene between the angry rioters, and the black citizens fleeing for safety. The rioters wanted destroy all evidence of interracial relations and businesses in the city – and they began attacking brothels, boarding houses, tenements, dance halls – any business that catered to black citizens. Some places got entirely destroyed, while other rioters went to the white owners of the businesses, and tore their clothing from their bodies.

While most women and children were spared being murdered, the rioters went after mainly black men during the attacks. They tortured, burned them, hung them, and even sexually attacked them. Rioters at the waterfront hung William Jones, before burning his body. They also attacked dock worker Charles Jackson – nearly drowning him to death, before moving on to Jeremiah Robinson. He was beaten to death, and his body was thrown into the river. Another man, William Williams, was attacked by a crowd of men, women, and children – and he was stabbed, then stoned to death. Nobody intervened in his attack.

Black coachman Abraham Franklin was forcibly removed from his apartment, and dragged to a lamp post where he was lynched. The crowd cheered for Jefferson Davis – the Confederate president. The terrifying attacks continued throughout the night. Some black residents tried to protest, or defend themselves, but the crowds were merciless. After James Costello fired a gun at one attacker before trying to flee, he was assaulted by six white men, who beat and kicked him, before hanging him from a lamp post.

The Longshoreman's Association (a white labour union) started to patrol the piers during the riot, proclaiming that they wanted to eradicate the black workers from the industry. Other industries, however, were also trying to rid themselves of black workers (including skilled artisans, hack drivers, and cartmen). The riot continued on, as mobs of working-class New Yorkers fought to remove black citizens from worksites, housing, even entire neighbourhoods.

Many believe that the journalists who had written sensationalist stories about the evils of interracial relationships and businesses, had achieved their goal of convincing lower-class residents (particularly Irish) that there must be a divide between black and white people, and that the freed slaves and other black populations were somehow lesser than.

Five Points, considered one of the most well-known interracial areas of New York, was surprisingly quiet throughout the riot. The mobs didn't go after brothels in the area, and they didn't kill any black residents in those borders.

At one point, the mob attacked black drugstore owner Philip White, who worked at the corner of Gold and Frankfurt Street. His Irish neighbours, however, sent the mob packing, as Philip White was known to give credit to many of his clients, and even extending it when locals were short on money.

The Irish gangs had focused their anger against the police and troops. Because of this, the Bowery Boys (and other nativist gangs) went to Five Points, and wreaked havoc on the area. They attacked residents, and destroyed homes and businesses, taking advantage of the Irish gang's temporary absence in the low-income neighbourhood.

Rioters attacked Hart's Alley, and when they were trapped at the dead end, the rioters were attacked by black and white residents who lived above the alley. They poured hot starch on the rioters, and forced them out of the area. These sorts of incidents were few and far between in Five Points, in comparison to the rest of the city.

Five Points was not the only area to be quiet during the riot. Company 33 ('Black Joke' Engine Company) that had been present during the beginning of the riot, returned to their neighbourhood and didn't participate any further. The German community, who had been active during the beginning of the riot, also stepped out of the remaining riot. The Germans, who mainly lived in the immigrant community called Kleindeutschland (located between Division Street, and 14th Street), was quiet for the rest of the riot.

Some neighbourhoods formed vigilance groups to prevent looting and rioting in their area, and there were a great deal of civilians who volunteered to help the police protect their neighbourhoods. There were also reports of politicians, as well as Catholic priests going around and talking to the rioters, hoping to find a peaceful resolution between police, and the rioters. Some politicians had even offered to buy men out of the draft.

Five Points, and Corlears Hook had been instantly presumed to be the worst areas during the draft riots. But that was not how things turned out at all. Five Points was quiet, and it was believed that this occurred because the area had a lot of brothels, saloons, and gangs. It was believed that the gangs who lived there, had made sure to keep the area peaceful.

During the riots, many landlords decided that in order to ensure the safety of their rental properties, they needed to drive out their black tenants. Many of the black community left the city, or went into hiding during the riots, fearing that they would be attacked and murdered as well.

One of the black-owned businesses that was destroyed by the rioters, was James McCune Smith's pharmacy at 93 West Broadway, which was believed to have been the first owned by a black man in the United States.

In total, eleven black men were tragically lynched throughout the five-day riot. One of the eleven victims that had been killed that night, was a seven-year-old boy – nephew of Bermudian First Sergeant Robert John Simmons, of the 54th Massachusetts Infantry Regiment. Simmons' account of the fighting in South Carolina (which had been written on the approach to Fort Wagner on July 18, 1863), was later published on December 23, 1863, in the *New York Tribune*. Simmons had died in August, succumbing to the wounds he'd received in the attack on Fort Wagner.

It was the general consensus that black women were left alone – unless they tried to defend their husbands (and then they, too, were attacked and beaten). One man tried to protect himself, by dressing in his wife's clothing, in order to escape violence. Jeremiah Robinson was recognized, unfortunately. The mob attacked him, and murdered him. They allowed his wife to leave, and she travelled to Brooklyn.

Hundreds of citizens fled the city, fearing for their personal safety. Albro Lyons, the keeper of the Coloured Sailor's Home, did his best to protect the boardinghouse on the first day of the riots. But as things quickly escalated, Lyons travelled to the local police station. He asked for an escort out of the city for his wife and family, and was accompanied by an officer to the Sailors' Home to grab as many belongings as he could. Lyons and his family boarded the Roosevelt Street ferry, then went to Williamsburg, in Brooklyn. Lyons knew that as soon as he boarded the ferry, it would be the last time that he ever would step foot in New York City. Other residents travelled to New Jersey, while some travelled even further to escape the riots, and the racism running rampant in the city. By 1865, the city's black population had fallen drastically to under ten thousand people – which was the lowest it had been since 1820.

Monday night brought heavy rain to the area, which sent some of the rioters scattering, as well as putting out some of the fires. The next morning, however, the crowds returned in full force. Abby Hopper Gibbons, daughter of abolitionist Isaac Hopper, had her house burned down because she supported black residents. There were white amalgamationists like Ann Derrickson, and Ann Martin – both of whom were married to black men – who were attacked during the riot. Mary Burke, a white sex worker who catered to black clientele, was also attacked during these five days.

On Tuesday the 14th, Governor Seymour performed his famous 'My Friends' speech, as he stood on the front steps of New York City Hall.

Seymour was not a big fan of Lincoln's war policies, and some people believed that Seymour was a 'copperhead' (a grass-roots movement of Democrats who were against the Civil War, and wanted to create a peace settlement with the Confederates). They described him as 'an agitator who was being disloyal'. Despite his misgivings towards some of Lincoln's war policies, he hurried to the City Hall to try and restore order.

Seymour spoke out to the crowd, who were mainly Irish rioters. Seymour had questioned Lincoln about the constitutionality of the Emancipation Proclamation, and had been opposed to the federal draft – believing that it was a violation of states' rights. He was sympathetic towards the rioters, as he spoke out to them during his speech. He told that he believed the Conscription Act was unconstitutional. The reason why his speech was dubbed 'My Friends', was because that was how he addressed the rioters as they stood at the City Hall steps. This speech, and his opposition views towards Lincoln, led Republicans to brand him as a Confederate, and to think of him as treasonous. Seymour's political career suffered after the Draft Riots, as he was later defeated in the re-election against Republican Reuben Fenton. General Ulysses S. Grant beat him in the Presidential election, and Seymour later became an elder Democratic Party statesman.

President Lincoln had to divert militia regiments, as well as volunteer troops from the Battle of Gettysburg, so that they could try and control the riots happening in New York City. General John E. Wool brought about 800 soldiers and Marines to the city – from forts in West Point, Brooklyn Navy Yard, and New York Harbour. The militias were ordered to return to New York.

The military reached the city on the second day, and by that time the mobs had already ransacked and destroyed a great deal of public buildings. They had also wrecked two Protestant churches, many black homes and businesses, the black orphanage, and many homes of sympathizers. Tensions were growing stronger, especially as many members of the black community had been injured, murdered, or driven from the city. A great deal of black-owned businesses, and houses were destroyed. The riots were violent, extremely dangerous, and chaotic.

When the mobs were destroying buildings on Second Avenue, Colonel Henry O'Brien, and 150 men from the Eleventh New York Volunteers arrived on scene with 200 police officers. The crowds were massive, and they were out of control. O'Brien ordered his men to shoot their guns into the air, and to load the two cannons with blanks. The loud noises from the cannon managed to quiet the crowd somewhat, but there were two unfortunate deaths – two young children who had been up on the rooftop were killed.

O'Brien decided to return home, as he lived nearby. His home had been looted, though his family was unharmed. He arrived home by two that afternoon. Unfortunately, rioters saw him arrive, and they attacked him. O'Brien was tortured and murdered in front of his house, attacked by a mob of men, women, and boys.

Wednesday the 15th saw some improvement, when Robert Nugent (assistant provost-marshal-general) was given word by his superior officer, Colonel James Barnet Fry, to postpone the draft. The story was quickly picked up by newspapers, and some of the rioters were satisfied with the draft postponement, and decided to head home.

As the militias started to enter New York, they still had to fight against the remaining protesters, many of whom were still intent on destroying property, and attacking civilians. Governor Seymour, and General Wood holed up in the St. Nicholas Hotel, making it their headquarters during the riot. Major General John E. Wool, who was the commander of the Department of the East, stated on July 16th that *'Martial law ought to be proclaimed, but I have not a sufficient force to enforce it'*.

Police were exhausted from the past few days of fighting the rioters. They had only been armed with batons and pistols, and they were greatly relieved when soldiers arrived by boat or train – armed with muskets and cannons. The soldiers were prepared to take down as many rioters as they could.

Wednesday ended with a bloodbath on East 19th Street, where the police had been trying to contain the crowd. The approaching army patrol had been mobbed, and the soldiers started to shoot several rounds of grape shot from their cannon, striking several members of the crowd. But they were quickly overwhelmed, as snipers began shooting at the soldiers from the windows and rooftops, trying to take out as many as they could.

Some of the soldiers went into the surrounding buildings, seeking out the snipers to take them down. The commander was not comfortable with the level of violence, and so he forced the soldiers to retreat. They were not even able to take their wounded soldiers with them. It was only when a second wave of soldiers arrived, that the wounded were rescued.

Thursday the 16th, the New York State Militia, and other federal troops had arrived in the city. This included the 152nd New York Volunteers, 26th Michigan Volunteers, the 27th Indiana Volunteers, and the 7th Regiment New York State Militia from Frederick, Maryland. The governor also sent in the 74th and 65th regiments from the New York State Militia, though they hadn't been in federal service, as well as part of the 20th Independent Battery, New York Volunteer Artillery from Fort Schuyler, in Throggs Neck.

That Thursday, The *New York Times* reported that the Plug uglies, and Blood Tubs (both nativist gangs from Baltimore, Maryland), had travelled to New York to participate in the riots. There were mention of other gangs, such as the Scuykill Rangers, and other groups travelling to the area from Philadelphia, to fight along the Dead Rabbits, and Macherelvillers. The *New York Times* also wrote the following: '*the scoundrels cannot afford to miss this golden opportunity of indulging their brutal natures, and at the same time serving their colleagues the Copperheads and secessionist sympathizers*'.

The New York State Militia were the first of the military groups to arrive. Thousands of militia, and Federal troops were in the city. People were fighting, buildings still being looted or threatened, and the militia had a difficult time maintaining order.

Thursday saw its share of fighting and destruction, but it also had some residents return to work. Factories started to open again, streetcars were up and running, and telegraph communications had begun again. Railroads were beginning their regular service after repairs were done, and there was a much larger police and military presence on the streets to ensure that everything would run smoothly.

Members of the black community started to come out of hiding, hoping that the increased police numbers would ensure their safety. Some returned to their homes. Though there were still attacks on the streets where black people were at risk of being beaten, the police were able to chase off their attackers. Thursday saw another death of a black man – who had been thrown into the East River and drowned.

On the upper East Side, rioters had built barricades, trying desperately to keep out the police and soldiers. They were able to fight off the first wave of soldiers. But the second group of soldiers that arrived were much bigger in numbers, and things quickly escalated. Soldiers started to break into nearby houses, seeking out the rioters. From house to house, the soldiers broke in and fought off as many of the protesters as they could. Many of the rioters had been known to say 'Better to die at home, than in Virginia'. These words were ones they took to heart, as many of them rioters ended up getting killed. Eventually, the military was able to clear out the entire protest, and the streets were returned to normalcy.

On the night of the 16th, the final confrontation between rioters and soldiers, took place near Gramercy Park. There were a dozen deaths that night, between the rioters, police, and members of the militia.

The troops were finally able to regain control of the city, but unfortunately, there had been a large amount of dead or injured people, and property damage. The total death toll was 119, and there were more than 300 injured people (many of them soldiers, or police). The exact numbers are unclear, as it is believed that a great deal of deaths went unreported. It may have been because people were holding secret burials, so that the local police would not be aware of their family's connection with the riots. Others believe that bodies were dumped in the river to dispose of them.

There was a massive amount of property damage from the riot. It totaled about 1-5 million dollars (which in today's market, would be from 16-87 million dollars). The city treasure later indemnified a quarter of that amount.

New York Republicans wanted the Democrats to be brought up on charges of treason, and conspiracy. The Lincoln administration, however, refused to bring them up on charges – instead, they left it up to local authorities to deal with the aftermath. Democrats were extremely reluctant to prosecute any of their voters, and so very few of the rioters actually got any serious crime indictments. A few rioters had been charged with looting, but that was it. The people who had murdered Abraham Franklin, Henry O'Brien, and so many others went unpunished.

Some historians, including Samuel Eliot Morison, believe that the Draft Riots in New York essentially were equivalent to a Confederate victory.

There were more than fifty buildings burned to the ground, which included the police stations, the Protestant churches, and the orphanage. Thousands of troops had to be pulled from the Gettysburg Campaign to keep order in the city, and those troops could've aided hunting down the war-weary Army of Northern Virginia, as they retreated from the Union.

For the black residents that decided to stay, there were organizations (such as Union League Club, and the Committee of Merchants for the Relief of Coloured People), that collected forty thousand dollars, and handed money out to about 2,500 riot victims. They needed to find new jobs, as well as housing after the riot. The white elite of New York organized relief for black riot victims, and tried to help many of them find jobs, and housing, as a great deal of them had been evicted during the riots.

On August 19, the government decided to resume the draft in New York. They managed to finish it in ten days' time, without any riots this time. There were less men drafted than had been anticipated, and the working class were surprised at the low numbers. From the 750,000 men chosen throughout the United States, only 45,000 men were sent into active duty.

A great deal of people were still angered by the government's decision to do the draft, and the use of federal power or martial law to enforce it. A great deal of rich Democratic businessmen fought the government, saying that the draft was unconstitutional. Tammany Democrats didn't seek to call the draft unconstitutional, but instead helped drafted men pay the commutation fees.

By December 1863, black citizens formed an alliance with Republicans. The secretary of war gave the Union League Club permission to raise a black regiment. The club decided to march the resident through the New York streets to the Hudson River, where they would board a ship to the south. The regiment had more than a thousand members.

More than a hundred thousand people lined the streets to watch the first black regiment march through the city, dressed in fine blue uniforms, white gloves, and white leggings. The parade included the police superintendent, a hundred police officers, the Union League Club, a band, and many supporters of the regiment.

The parade hoped to show to the city, that black residents were equal to their white neighbours, and that it was a time of change. Though they tried their best to keep spirits high, and fight against the racial tensions that had occurred during the draft riot, the regiment was still met with some pushback.

Some reported that although it was supposed to be a 'black regiment', there were some mixed-race soldiers marching in the parade. Others commented heavily on the soldiers' loyalty to the union, and how they were well-behaved, without drinking heavily, or disobeying orders. The parade held mixed reviews from different viewpoints, as some New Yorkers were still harbouring resentment towards the black community post-riot.

The creation of the all-black regiment was definitely a step in the right direction, but New York (and the country as a whole) continued to have racial issues for more than a century. Even in the twenty-first century, the city is still suffering from huge racial inequalities, and the black community have lost a substantial amount of people to racist attacks simply for the colour of their skin.

Gradually, Southern support declined in the city, and the support for the Union became stronger. New York banks eventually financed the Civil War, and the state's industries started to strengthen – until they were more productive than the entire Confederacy. By the end of the war, more than 450,000 soldiers, militia, and sailors had enlisted from New York State. Out of those men, 46,000 men from the state died, some from fighting in the war and becoming wounded, while many more died from diseases.

DEAD RABBITS IN POP CULTURE

Henry Sherman Backus, and Daniel Decatur Emmett wrote a song about the Dead Rabbits' battle with the Bowery Boys on July 4th, 1857. In their lyrics, they describe the gang members rolling up their sleeves as they prepared for battle on Bayard Street, and how they fought well into the night. Some were wounded, others were killed. Blood was spilled on both sides, and how they used bricks, clubs, and guns to fight their opposers.

George Henry Hall painted 'A Dead Rabbit' in 1858 (though it should be noted, that it also goes by the name 'Study of the Nude', or 'Study of an Irishman'). The painting depicts one of the Dead Rabbits that were killed during the July 4th riot.

In 1998, History Channel's documentary series 'History's Mysteries' had a feature about the Dead Rabbit Riot. This was not the first time that the Rabbits were featured on screen. Martin Scorsese's 2002 film 'Gangs of New York, (which was inspired by Herbert Asbury's book of the same title), featured the Dead Rabbits, Hellcat Maggie, and the Bowery Boys.

The 2014 film 'Winter's Tale' also featured the Dead Rabbits, and the Short Tails. It was based on the 1983 Mark Helprin novel of the same title. The TV show 'Hell on Wheels' featured a few Dead Rabbit characters in their fourth season.

In 1915, a poetry book written by Richard Griffin was titled 'The Dead Rabbit Riot, A.D 1857: And Other Poems'. Patricia Beatty wrote a historical children's fiction novel in 1987, titled 'Charlie Skedaddle'. The book featured a Bowery Boy protagonist, but also mentioned Dead Rabbit characters. MacKinlay Kantor's 1955 novel 'Andersonville' featured the Dead Rabbits in one of his chapters.

WHAT REMAINS OF THE AREA?

In 1842, Charles Dickens toured the Five Points. In his book, 'American Notes for General Circulation', he described the area as: '*All that is loathsome, dropping and decayed in here*'. He had also written: '*nearly every house is a low tavern. Lances and alleys, paved with mud knee-deep, underground chambers, where they dance and game – hideous tenements which take their name from robbery and murder*'.

In New York's Civil Centre, the area is covered with giant classical structures – the pillars of New York court rooms. Columbus Park, a beautiful section of Chinatown. Under all these iconic and important parts of New York City, lies the buried remains of Five Points. It had been razed, and flattened in 1811.

Orange Street (Baxter), Cross Street (Mosco), Anthony Street (Worth), these streets had all formed 'Paradise Square'. It was an intersection that signified you were in Five Points, and the Sixth Ward. The area that during the nineteenth century, had been considered the most notorious district in the city, possibly even in the whole world. It was a low-class area, filled with immigrants and working class people. People would go there to drink, to gamble, to fight, to hire prostitutes.

PHOTO GALLERY

An illustration of the 'Astor Place Riot', which took place at the Astor Place Opera-House, on May 10, 1849. The riot left at least 22 rioters dead, and more than 120 people injured. It was a riot between immigrants, and nativists, and resulted in the largest number of civilian casualties due to military action in the US since the American Revolutionary War.

An illustrated sketch of a 'Dead Rabbit' gang member, holding a brickbat as a weapon. The sketch appeared in the July 18, 1857 edition of Frank Leslie's illustrated newspaper. It was from a riot scene in the Sixth Ward, between the Bowery Boys, and the Dead Rabbits, where men and women threw brickbats down at the police.

An illustrated sketch of a fight between the Dead Rabbits, and the Bowery Boys, in the 1857 Dead Rabbits Riot. The sketch appeared in the July 18 1857 edition of Frank Leslie's illustrated newspaper.

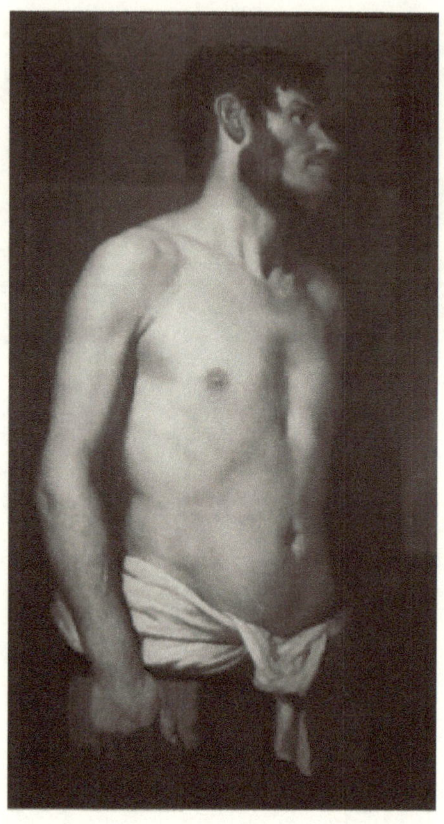

'A Dead Rabbit' is an 1858 painting by George Henry Hall, which also goes by the name 'Study of the Nude', or the 'Study of an Irishman'. The painting depicts a deceased Dead Rabbit member, that had been killed during the Dead Rabbit riot on July 4, 1857 in the Lower East Side.

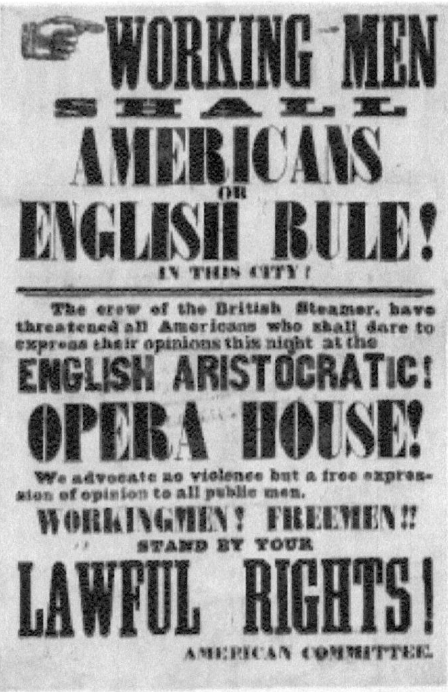

The above is a handbill produced by Ned Buntline, and the American Committee, that was handed out before the Astor Place Riot in 1849.

An illustration of the Astor Place Riot, that occurred in 1849. The illustration was from the 'Recollections of a New York chief of Police: an official record of thirty-eight years as patrolman, detective, captain, inspector and chief of New York Police'. The book was written by George W. Walling, and published in 1887.

The illustration shows the fight between the rioters, and the militia during the Astor Place Riot. It was published in 1882.

The coloured illustration above was by F. S Chanfrau, depicting the 'Mose' character in 1848. The Nativist Bowery Boys gang would wear their volunteer fireman uniforms, with black stovepipe top hats to show their gang colours.

The above illustration depicts the looting that took place during 1863 Draft Riot, as well as the Colored Orphan Asylum that had been burned down.

The above illustration depicts Governor Seymour delivering his famous 'My Friends' speech on the steps of New York's City Hall, during the second day of the Draft Riots in 1863. It is believed that the illustration was drawn by Henry L. Stephens, from New York.

The above illustration appeared in William J. Bradley's 'The Civil War: Fort Sumter to Appomatox'. It depicts rioters attacking and setting a building on fire, on Lexington Avenue, during the New York Draft Riot in 1863.

An illustration of the 'Battle of the Barricades' during the New York Draft Riots. The image was published in 'recollections of a New York chief of Police: an official record of thirty-eight years as patrolman, detective, captain, inspector, and chief of New York Police'. The book was published in 1887, authored by George W. Walling.

John Morrissey, an immigrant from County Tipperary, Ireland, was gang leader of the Dead Rabbits. He was also a boxer, and a gambler. He later ran for Congress, backed by Tammany Hall. He served two terms.

The above illustration, titled 'A Dog Fight at Kit Burns', was illustrated by Edward Winslow Martin. The image depicts the rat-pit, at Sportsmen's Hall, and was published in James McCabe's 'The Secrets of the Great City' in Philadelphia, 1868.